CW00520060

The Qur'anic Treasures

Khurram Murad

The Islamic Foundation

Published by
The Islamic Foundation,
Markfield Dawah Centre,
Ratby Lane, Markfield,
Leicester LE67 9RN, UK

Quran House, PO Box 30611, Nairobi, Kenya

PMB 3193, Kano, Nigeria

First published 1997

ISBN 0 86037 274 X

British Library Cataloguing in Publication Data
A Catalogue card for this book is available from the British Library

Typeset in Baskerville 11/14

Printed and bound in Great Britain by the Cromwell Press

Preface

What does the Qur'an have to say?

This should be important to know for all who are concerned with humanity and peace in this world, torn apart by strife, hatred and violence. It should be important whether one believes that the Qur'an is the Word of God or not.

To know what the Qur'an says is important because the Qur'an has made a deep and abiding impact on the course of human civilization and history in many fundamental ways; because it has been inspiring, shaping, governing, and directing countless human lives over the ages, since it first appeared fourteen hundred years ago. And, it still does.

The Qur'an, among all other books believed to be divine, is the only book which itself claims, and is believed by its followers, to be *literally* the word of God. Those who first heard it from the lips of the Prophet Muhammad had absolutely no doubt that, through him, God was speaking to them. It totally transformed them: it quickened their hearts, it reshaped their minds; it made their eyes overflow with tears and their bodies tremble with awe, it changed them into new individuals, as well as a new society and polity; it led them to be the leaders of mankind and founders of a rich and flowering civilization.

More significantly, what a remarkable testimony it is to the unique power of the Qur'an that, in an age when God has been made irrelevant to human existence and concerns, millions and millions of human beings – as much as one fifth of the human race – still cling tenaciously to the book which they believe with certainty to be the Word of God, as the only blueprint for a bright, progressive, postmodern future. It is still the supreme source of inspiration, guidance and comfort in their spiritual, moral, social and cultural lives, it still influences and shapes their ways of thinking and conduct, both private and public, in innumerable ways.

To know what it has to say is therefore not only important for better inter-human understanding and amity, but it may be crucial for the destiny of mankind too.

However, everyone cannot venture to read the whole of the Qur'an, though its length is less than that of the New Testament. Yet everyone should have the opportunity to taste the delicious fruits in the garden of the Qur'an.

The Quranic Treasures is a small step towards the fulfilment of the enormous task of making the words of the Qur'an heard in our times. This pocket-size, short book is an anthology of its selected verses, arranged under various topics. Though an anthology by its very nature has to leave out much precious and important material, these selections, it is hoped, will give even the unfamiliar and the uninitiated a good glimpse of the vast treasures of knowledge and wisdom offered in the Qur'an, and will bring them face to face with the light that the Qur'an is.

This short pocket book, it is also hoped, may spur and tempt the readers to take up the reading of the whole of the Qur'an. Even the believers may find it a useful companion for keeping in touch with the Qur'anic teachings and making them heard in our times.

Finally, I pray to Allah, *subhanahu wa ta'ala,* to accept this humble endeavour in the cause of his great and majestic book, forgive my shortcomings and mistakes, and grant me to live by what he says.

Leicester   **Khurram Murad**
26 Rajab 1417
7 December 1996

1

The Human Cry

All praise be to God alone,
the Lord of all the worlds,
the All-Merciful, the Ever
Mercy-giving,
the Master of the Day of
Judgement.
You alone we worship, and You
alone we ask for help.
Guide us on the Straight Path,
the path of those whom You
have blessed, not of those who
incur Your anger, nor of those
who go astray

(*al-Fātiḥah* 1: 1–7)

2

The Mystery of Life
Where to Find the Light

God the Light, that Shines Forever

God is the Light of the heavens and the earth.

The parable of His Light is like a niche wherein is a lamp; the lamp is in a glass – the glass shines like a radiant star – [a lamp] lit from a blessed tree, an olive tree that is neither of the east nor of the west, whose oil would well-nigh give light even if no fire touched it; light upon light! God guides to His Light whom He wills. …

And as for those who choose to deny [God], their deeds are like a mirage in a desert, which the thirsty supposes to be water, till, when he comes to it, he finds it is nothing; instead there he finds God with him, and He pays him his account in full. Indeed God is swift in reckoning.

Or, like the depths of darkness upon an abysmal sea, made yet more dark by wave billowing above wave, above which are clouds: depths of darkness, piled one upon another, [so much so that] when one holds up his hand, he can hardly see it: [thus] to whomsoever God gives no light, he has no light (al-Nūr 24: 35–40).

God the Sustainer, Who Provides Everything

Now, all the [false gods] are an enemy to me, except the Lord of all the worlds: it is He who has created me, and so it is He who guides me; it is He who gives me to eat and drink, and whenever I am sick it is He who heals me; and it is He who makes me to die and then will bring me to life. And upon Him, I pin my hope that He would forgive my sins on the Day of Judgement (al-Shuʿarā' 26: 77–82).

The Light that is Life

Can, then, one who was dead and whom We gave life, and for whom We set up a light whereby he lives among men, be like the one who is in deep darkness, out of which he cannot come out? (*al-An'ām* 6: 122).

The Luminous Book

There has come to you from God a light and a luminous Book, through which God, by His grace, guides all who seek His good pleasure on the path of peace, and brings them out of the depths of darkness into light and guides them onto a Straight Path (*al-Mā'idah* 5: 15–16).

And thus [O Muhammad] We have revealed to you the life-giving Message at Our behest. [Before this Message came to you] you did not know what the Book is, nor what the faith [implies]. But now We have made this [Message] the light, whereby We guide among Our servants whom We will, so [with this light] you indeed guide onto the Straight Path – the path of God, to whom belongs all that is in the heavens and all that is on earth. Surely, with God is the beginning and the end of all things (*al-Shūrā* 42: 52–3).

O mankind, there has now come to you an exhortation from your Lord, and a healing for all the ills in hearts, and a guidance and a mercy to all the believers.

Say: In this bounty of God and in His mercy – in this, then – let them rejoice: it is better than whatever (worldly wealth) they may amass (*Yūnus* 10: 57–8).

3

Is the Qur'an the Word of God?

Say: 'Does any of those you make gods beside God guide to the truth?' Say: 'It is God alone who guides to the truth. Which, then, is more worthy to be followed: He who guides to the truth, or he who cannot find the right way unless he is guided? What then ails you, how do you judge?'

Indeed most people follow only conjecture, but conjecture can never be a substitute for truth. Surely God knows all they do.

This Qur'an is such as could not possibly have been composed by anyone except God: it confirms what was revealed before it, and spells out fully [the contents of] the Book, which – let there be no doubt about it – comes from the Lord of all the worlds.

And yet they say, 'He [Muhammad] has forged it'! Say: 'Produce, then, a single *Sūrah* [chapter] like the Qur'an, and call to your aid anyone you can, other than God, if what you say is true' (*Yūnus* 10: 35–8).

Those who have chosen to deny the truth say, 'This [Qur'an] is nothing but a forgery which he [Muhammad] has himself concocted, and certain people have helped him in this.' These people pervert the truth and indulge in falsehood. They say, 'These are legends of ancient times, which he has got written down, and they are read out to him morning and evening.' Say, 'He who has sent it down knows all the mysteries of the heavens and the earth. He is All-forgiving, All-mercy-giving.' They also say, 'What sort of Messenger is this who eats food [like all other mortals] and goes about in the market-places? Why has no angel been sent with him, to act as a warner along with him? Or, why has not a treasure been given to him? Or, at least, he should have had a garden to eat of?'

And so these evil-doers say, 'If you were to follow

[Muhammad] you would be following only a human-being, who is under a spell' (*al-Furqān* 25: 4–8).

Will they not, then, try to understand this Qur'an? Had it come from anyone other than God, they would have found in it many an inner contradiction (*al-Nisā'* 4: 82).

No! I call to witness all that you see, as well as all that you do not see! This [Qur'an] is indeed the word [brought] by a noble Messenger. It is not the word of a poet, but little do you [want] to believe; and neither is it the word of a soothsayer, but little do you [want] to take it to heart. [It has been] sent down by the Lord of all the worlds (*al-Ḥāqqah* 69: 38–43).

And when Our clear messages are conveyed to them, they – those who do not expect meeting Us – say, 'Bring a Qur'an other than this, or alter this one.' Say, 'It is not within my power to alter it of my own accord. I follow nothing, except what is revealed to me. Truly, I would dread, were I to rebel against my Lord, the punishment of a dreadful day.'

Say, 'Had God [not] willed, I would not have brought this [book] to you, neither would He have brought it to your knowledge. Indeed, a whole lifetime I have dwelt among you before this [Book came to me]: will you not, then, use your reason?' (*Yūnus* 10: 15–16).

Had We so willed, We could indeed take away whatever We have revealed to you, and in that case you would find none to protect you against Us. [Whatever you receive is] only by the mercy of your Lord; His favour to you is great indeed.

Say, 'If all mankind and all jinn come together to produce the like of this Qur'an, they would never produce its like, even though they help one another [to their best]' (*al-Isrā'* 17: 86–8).

Why no Miracles?

And they say, '[O Muhammad] We will not believe you till you make a spring gush forth from the earth for us; or till you own a garden of date-palms and vines, and you make rivers of water to flow abundantly; or till you make skies to fall down upon us, as you threaten, in fragments, or till you bring God and angels face to face before us; or till you have a house made of gold; or till you go up into heaven; but nay, we would never believe even in your going up till you bring down to us a book which we ourselves could read.'

Say, 'Glory be to my Lord! Am I anything but a mortal man, a Messenger?' Indeed nothing has prevented people [more] from believing whenever God's guidance came to them [through a prophet] but that they objected, 'Would God have sent a mere human being as Messenger?' Say, 'Had there been angels walking about on earth as their natural abode, We would indeed have sent to them an angel out of heaven as Messenger.'

Say, 'God suffices as witness [to my truthfulness] between me and you, surely He is aware of and sees His servants (al-Isrā' 17: 90–5).

4

Why Divine Guidance?

Why Life, the Existential Question

Blessed is He in whose hands is the Kingdom –
who is powerful over everything – who has created
death and life, so that He might test you as to which
among you [proves that he] is good in conduct (*al-
Mulk* 67: 1–2).

Has there [not] been a long time when man was
not even a mentionable thing. It is We who have
created man out of a sperm-drop intermingled, so
that We might test him. And therefore We have made
him hearing and seeing. Surely We have guided him
to the way [and it rests with him to prove himself]
either grateful or ungrateful (*al-Dahr* 76: 1–2).

Free-will and Moral Responsibility

Say: The Truth has come from your Lord. Let him who will, believe it, and let him who will, reject it (*al-Kahf* 18: 29).

Whosoever chooses to follow guidance, follows it for his own good; whosoever goes astray, goes astray to his own loss (*al-Isrā'* 17: 15).

And [look at the witness] by the human self, and how suitably has He formed it [to fulfil its purpose in life], and then imbued it with [tendencies for] evil as well as good; successful is he who develops his self [in goodness], and failed is he who buries it [in evil-doing] (*al-Shams* 91: 7–9).

Accountability and Judgement

Has [man] not been told of what was written in the books of Moses, and in those of Abraham who fulfilled his every duty: that no person shall be made to bear the burden of another; and that nothing shall be accounted unto a person except what he does himself; and that in time he shall see the results of his doings; and then he shall be recompensed for them with the fullest recompense (*al-Najm* 53: 36–41).

They say, 'There is nothing beyond our present life. We die as we come to life, and nothing but time destroys us.' But of this they have no knowledge whatever, they merely speculate. And when Our messages, clear messages, are recited to them, their only argument is this: 'Bring us our forefathers [as witnesses] if what you claim is true.'

Say, 'It is God who gives you life, then makes you die; and in the end He shall gather you on the Day of Resurrection [the coming of] which is beyond all doubt, but most people do not understand.'

To God belongs the kingdom of the heavens and the earth. And on the Day when the Last Hour is come – on that Day all those who refused to believe [this Day] shall be the real losers. And you shall see all people hobbling on their knees, [for] all people will be called upon to [face] their record: 'Today you shall be recompensed for all that you ever did. This is Our record, it speaks about you in all truth; for We had been recording all that you were doing.'

Now for those who have believed and done righteous deeds, their Lord will admit them into His mercy – that, that is the manifest success.

But to those who denied [it will be said]: 'Were not My messages recited to you, but you gloried in your arrogance, and thus you became a sinful people. For when it was said [to you], "God's promise is true, and there can be no doubt about [the coming of] the Last Hour", you would answer, "We do not know what that Last Hour may be: We think it is no more than an idle speculation, and we are by no means convinced" '.

And [on that Day] the evil of their doings will become obvious to them and they will be overwhelmed by the very thing which they were wont to deride. And [they] will be told: 'Today We shall forget you as you have been forgetful of meeting Us on this Day, and now your refuge is the Fire, and you have none to help you' (al-Jāthiyah 45: 24–34).

Prophethood and Divine Guidance

We have sent revelation to you as We sent revelation to Noah, and the prophets after him, as We sent revelation to Abraham, Ishmael, Isaac, Jacob, and their descendants, including Jesus, Job, Jonah, Aaron, and Solomon, and We gave David Psalms – of some Messengers before you We have told you, of others We have not – and God spoke to Moses as well.

Messengers who gave good tidings as well as warnings, so that mankind, after the coming of Messengers, would have no excuse before God [on the Judgement Day]; God is All-mighty, All-wise (*al-Nisā'* 4: 163–5).

[And God said to Adam] 'Get you all down out of it; yet there shall most certainly come to you guidance from Me, and those who follow My guidance need have no fear, and neither shall they grieve' (*al-Baqarah* 2: 38).

The Prophet to All Mankind Forever

Surely We have sent you [O Muhammad] with the Truth, as a herald of good tidings and a warner; for there never were a people without a warner having come among them (*al-Fāṭir* 35: 24).

We have sent you to the entire mankind to give them good tidings, and warn them; but most people do not understand this (*Saba'* 34: 28).

Say [O Muhammad]: 'O mankind, verily I am the Messenger of God to all of you, [sent by Him] to whom belongs the kingdom of the heavens and the earth. There is no god but He. He alone gives life and makes to die.'

Believe, then, in God, and in His Messenger, the unlettered Prophet – who believes in God and His words; follow him, so that you find guidance (*al-A'rāf* 7: 158).

And [O Prophet] We have indeed sent you as a Mercy for all the worlds. Say, 'The message that I have been given is only this much: your God is the One and Only God; will you, then, surrender yourselves unto Him?' (al-Anbiyā' 21: 107–8).

5

Inter-faith Dialogue

Unity of Religion

Say: We believe in God, and in that which has been sent down on us, and that sent down on Abraham, Ishmael, Isaac, Jacob, and their descendants, and that which was given to Moses and Jesus, and was given to all the prophets, from their Lord; we make no distinction between any of them; and we surrender ourselves to God alone (*al-Baqarah* 2: 136).

Come to a Common Creed: One God

Say: 'O People of the Book, come to the creed common between us and you: that we worship and serve none but God, and that we shall make no gods beside Him; that we shall not take human beings as Lords other than God.' If they turn away, say: 'Bear witness that we have surrendered to God.'

O People of the Book, why do you dispute about Abraham? The Torah was not sent down, neither the Gospel, but after him. Will you not, then, use your reason? . . . Abraham was not a Jew, neither a Christian, but he was a *muslim*, (one who surrendered himself unto God) turning away from all false idols. And he made no gods beside God (*Āl 'Imrān* 3: 64–7).

The Right Choice

God said: With My punishment I afflict those whom I will, but My mercy embraces everything: so, I shall confer it on those who are God-fearing, pay the Alms, and believe in Our messages; those who shall follow the [last] Messenger, the unlettered Prophet, whom they find mentioned in the Torah and the Gospel [that are] with them – he enjoins them what is right and forbids them what is wrong, makes lawful to them the good things of life and forbids them the bad things, and releases them from their burdens and from the shackles that are upon them. So those who shall believe in him, honour him, help him, and follow the light that has been sent down with him, it is they who will find salvation and success (*al-Aʿrāf* 7: 156–7).

No Coercion

Let there be no coercion in matters of religion. The right way has become distinct from (the way of) error. So, whosoever rejects the powers of evil, and believes in God, has taken hold of a most firm, unfailing support. God is All-hearing, All-knowing (*al-Baqarah* 2: 256).

For every one of you We have appointed a law and a way. And had God so willed, He could have made all of you one [religious] community, but [He willed it otherwise] in order to test you in what He has given you. Vie, then, with one another in doing good. Unto God you all must return, and then He will tell you [the truth] about which you used to differ (*al-Mā'idah* 5: 48).

The Jews say, 'The Christians have no valid grounds'; the Christians say, 'The Jews have no valid grounds'; and both quote the Book [of God]. So do those who have no knowledge [of the Book] speak like them. But it is God who will decide between them on the Day of Resurrection about all on which they differ (*al-Baqarah* 2: 113).

6

The Straight Path

Say: Come, let me tell you what God has
forbidden you, 'Do not make any god beside Him;
and do good to your parents; and do not kill your
children for fear of poverty – for it is We who
provide sustenance to you, and [shall provide] to
them as well; and do not go near any shameful
deeds, be they open or secret; and do not take any
life, which it has been forbidden to take, except by
right: This He has enjoined upon you so that you
might use your reason.

'And do not touch the property of an orphan,
except in a fair manner, until he comes of age; give
full measure and weight [in all your dealings] with
justice; [however] We do not burden any person

with more than his capacity, and when you speak, be just, even though it be [against] a near kinsman. And fulfil your promise to God: This He has enjoined upon you, so that you might keep it in mind.'

And [know] that this is My Straight Path: follow it, then, and follow not diverse paths lest they scatter you from His path (*al-Anʿām* 6: 151–3).

Say: 'As for me, my Lord has guided me onto a straight path – the sound and perfect way of life, the way of Abraham, who turned away from all false gods and made no gods beside God.' Say: 'My Prayer, and all my acts of worship, and my living and my dying are for God alone, the Lord of all the worlds. He has no associate: Thus I have been commanded, and I am foremost among those who surrender themselves unto Him' (*al-Anʿām* 6: 161–3).

Whosoever holds fast to God, he has been guided onto the Straight Path (*Āl ʿImrān* 3: 101).

7

The Most Merciful, Creator, Sovereign, and Lord God

In His Presence

To God belongs the kingdom of the heavens and the earth; and God is powerful over everything.

Surely in the creation of the heavens and the earth, and in the succession of night and day, there are signs [of God] for all who possess insight, who [thereby] remember God whether they are standing, sitting, or lying, and when they reflect upon the creation of the heavens and the earth [cry out]: 'O our Lord, You have not created any of this without meaning and purpose. Glory be to You, keep us safe from the Fire' (*Āl ʿImrān* 3: 189–91).

It is We who have created man, and We know even whatever thoughts arise within him; and, We are nearer to him than his neck-vein. The two angels appointed to record, do record: one sitting on the right, and one on the left: Not a word he utters, but there is an observer with him, ready [to record it] (*Qāf* 50: 16–18).

And He is with you wherever you are; and God sees all that you do (*al-Ḥadīd* 57: 4).

Know the Only God

Say: He is God, the One and Unique;
God, the Eternal source and support
of everything;
He begets not, and neither is He begotten;
and none is His equal (*al-Ikhlāṣ* 112: 1–4).

Glory be to the Lord of the heavens and the earth, the Lord of the Throne, [He is] above all they may attribute to Him by way of definition [for, being the only Creator, His reality is utterly beyond any human comprehension, imagination or description, as it cannot be done without comparing the only Creator with the created] (*al-Zukhruf* 43: 82).

The Originator [is He] of the heavens and the earth. He has given you, of yourselves, mates – and also mates among the cattle – to multiply you thereby.

There is nothing like Him.

He is the All-hearing, the All-seeing. To Him belong the keys of the heavens and the earth. He grants His provision to whom He wills, in abundance or in scant measure. Surely He has knowledge of everything (*al-Shūrā* 42: 11–12).

This is God, your Lord; there is no god but He, the Creator of everything. So serve and worship Him alone, for He has everything in His care. No human vision can encompass Him, whereas He encompasses all human visions (*al-Anʿām* 6: 102–3).

Creation, Sustenance and Mercy

Can, then, He who creates be like any that cannot create? Will you not, then, take lesson? For should you try to count God's blessings, you would never compute them. God is indeed All-forgiving, All-compassionate .... And those they call upon, apart from God, can create nothing, since they themselves are created; they are dead, not alive, and do not even know when they shall be raised (al-Naḥl 16: 17–21).

O men, a parable is set forth, so give ear to it: surely those you call upon, instead of God, cannot create [as much as] a fly, even were they to join all their forces to that end. And if a fly robs them of anything, they cannot [even] rescue it from him. Weak is the seeker, and [weak] the sought! (al-Ḥajj 22: 73).

Or, [do they deny God?] Have they been created out of nothing? Or are they their own creators? Or, did they create the heavens and the earth? Nay, but they have no certainty of anything (al-Ṭūr 52: 35–6).

O mankind, worship and serve your Lord alone, who has created you and those who were before you, so that you may attain righteousness.

He has made for you the earth a resting place, and the sky a canopy, and has sent down water from the sky, and has thereby brought forth produce for your sustenance.

Do not, then, make anything as God's equal when you know (that He is One) (*al-Baqarah* 2: 21–2).

Verily your Lord is God.

He has created the heavens and the earth in six days, then sat Himself on the Throne. He covers the day with the night in swift pursuit. And the sun, and the moon, and the stars are all subservient by His command.

Surely, His is the creation, in Him rests the sovereignty. Blessed be God, the Lord of all the worlds.

Call on your Lord humbly, and in the secrecy of your hearts. Surely, He loves not transgressors. Do not spread corruption on earth, after it has been so well ordered. And call on Him with fear and longing. Surely, God's mercy is ever near to the doers of good (*al-Aʿrāf* 7: 54–6).

We create man out of the essence of clay, then We make him a drop of sperm in [the womb's] secure receptacle, then We create out of the drop a germ-cell, then We create out of the germ-cell an embryo, then We create within the embryo bones, then We clothe the bones with flesh – and then We bring this into being as a new creation. So blessed be God, the best of Creators!

Then, after all this, you shall surely die, and then on the Day of Resurrection you shall surely be raised from the dead (*al-Mu'minūn* 23: 12–16).

Perish man! How stubbornly does he deny the truth!

[Does he never think] out of what He has created him? Out of a drop of sperm! He creates him, then determines his nature, then makes it easy for him to live, and in the end makes him die, and so brings him to the grave, and then, when He wills, He shall raise him again to life. No indeed! Man has not fulfilled what He has enjoined upon him.

Let man, then, consider his food: We pour down rains abundantly, then We cleave the earth [with new growth], cleaving it asunder, then We make grain to grow out of it, and vines and edible plants, and olives, and date-palms, and gardens dense with foliage, and fruits, and pastures, for you and for your animals to enjoy (*'Abasa* 80: 17–32).

Your God is one God, there is no god but He, the Most Merciful, the Mercy-giving.

Surely in the creation of the heavens and the earth, in the succession of night and day, in the ships that sail through the sea with what benefits man, in the water God sends down from the sky, thereby giving life to the earth after it is dead and making all manner of living creatures to multiply thereon, in the change of the winds, and in the clouds between sky and earth which are harnessed – (in all this) surely there are messages for people who use their reason.

Yet there are people who make others as God's equals, loving them as only God should be loved; but those who have faith love God more than all else (*al-Baqarah* 2: 163–5).

Among His signs is that He has created you from dust; and, then, you became human beings scattered far and wide.

And among His signs is that He creates for you mates from among yourselves, so that you may live in tranquillity with them, and He has put love and mercy between you. Surely in this are messages for people who reflect.

And among His signs is the creation of the heavens and the earth, and the variations in your languages and your colours. Surely in this are messages for those who have knowledge.

And among His signs is your sleep at night or by day time, and your seeking of livelihood out of His bounty. Surely in this are messages for people who listen (*al-Rūm* 30: 20–3).

No God Beside God

Say, all praise belongs to God alone, and peace be upon His servants whom He has chosen (to be His Messengers). What, is God better, or gods they make beside God?

Look, who has created the heavens and the earth, and who sends down for you water from the skies – and therewith We make gardens of shining beauty to grow? It was not in your power to make any tree grow on earth. Is there a god with God? Nay, but they are people who swerve from the path of reason.

Or, who has made the earth a place fit to live in, who has made rivers in its midst, who has set upon it high mountains, and who has placed a barrier between two kinds of water? Is there a god with God? Nay, but most of them have no knowledge.

Or, who answers the distressed when he calls unto Him and relieves his suffering, and who makes you inherit the earth. Is there a god with God? Little indeed you remind yourselves.

Or, who guides you in darkness on land and sea, and sends the winds as a good tiding before the coming of His mercy? Is there a god with God?

High and exalted is God above gods they associate with Him.

Or, who creates all life in the first instance, and then brings it forth anew, and who gives you sustenance from heaven and earth? Is there a god with God? Say, 'Produce your evidence, if you are telling the truth' (*al-Naml* 27: 59–64).

Say: Have you thought about this? If God were to make the night continue over you without break, until the Day of Resurrection, what god other than God could bring you daylight? Will you not, then, listen?

Say: Have you thought about this? If God were to make the day continue over you without break, until the Day of Resurrection, what god other than God could bring you night in which you may rest? Will you not, then, see? (*al-Qaṣaṣ* 28: 72).

Say, who saves you from the dark dangers of land and sea, when you call upon Him humbly, and in the secrecy of your hearts, 'If You save us from this (danger), we shall surely be among the grateful.' Say, it is God who saves you, from this and from every other distress; and yet you make gods with God (*al-An'ām* 6: 63–4).

God-Man Relationship

All that is in the heavens and on earth glorifies God; He is the All-mighty, the All-wise.

To Him belongs the kingdom of the heavens and the earth; He gives life and death, and He has power over everything. He is the First and the Last, the Outward and the Inward; and He has knowledge of everything.

It is He who has created the heavens and the earth in six days, and, then, sat on the Throne. He knows all that enters the earth, and all that comes out of it, all that comes down from heaven, and all that goes up into it. And He is with you wherever you are. God sees all that you do.

To Him belongs the kingdom of the heavens and the earth; and all matters are returned unto God. He makes the night enter into day, and makes the day enter into night; and He knows all that is in hearts.

Attain faith in God and His Messenger, and

spend out of that which He has made you trustees. For, those of you who have faith and spend shall have a great reward (*al-Ḥadīd* 57: 1–7).

With Him are the keys of the Unseen, which none knows but He. And He knows whatever is on land and in the sea. Not a leaf falls but He knows it; neither is a grain in the earth's darkness, nor anything fresh or dry, but is recorded in (His) clear decree. It is He who causes you to be (like) dead by night, and knows all that you do in day time; and He brings you back to life each day, so that the appointed term be fulfilled; in the end, unto Him shall you return. Then He will tell you what you were doing (*al-Anʿām* 6: 59–60).

Say: O God, Lord of all power, You give power to whom You will, and You take away power from whom You will, and You give honour to whom You will, and You debase whom You will; in Your hand is all good, You have power over all things.

You make the night enter into the day, and the day enter into the night; You bring the living out of the dead, and the dead out of the living; and You give sustenance to whom You will, without measure (*Āl ʿImrān* 3: 26–7).

If God should touch you with misfortune, none can remove it but He; and if He should touch you with good fortune, He has power over everything. For He alone holds sway over His creatures; He is the All-wise, the All-aware (*al-Anʿām* 6: 17–18).

It is He who accepts repentance from His servants, and pardons bad deeds, and knows all that you do. And He answers those who have faith and do righteous deeds, and gives them – out of His bounty – far more (*al-Shūrā* 42: 25–6).

Say: O My servants who have transgressed against their own selves, despair not of God's Mercy; for God forgives all sins, surely He is the All-forgiving, the Mercy-giving.
So, turn to your Lord and surrender yourselves to Him, before the punishment comes upon you; for, then, you will not be helped (*al-Zumar* 39: 53–4).

8

Inter-human Relations

General

God enjoins justice, and compassion, and generous giving to the kinsfolk; and He forbids all indecent acts, all that is wrong, and all excesses against others. He exhorts you, so that you bear in mind.

Fulfil your pledge to God whenever you bind yourselves by a pledge; and break not the oaths, after they have been confirmed; for you have made God your surety and God knows all that you do (*al-Naḥl* 16: 90–1).

And speak to all people in a kindly way (*al-Baqarah* 2: 83).

Humility

The true servants of the Most Merciful are those who behave gently and with humility on earth, and whenever the foolish quarrel with them, they reply with [words of] peace (*al-Furqān* 25: 63).

Turn not your cheek away from people in scorn and pride, and walk not on earth haughtily; for God does not love anyone who acts proudly and boastfully. Be modest in your bearing and lower your voice; for the ugliest sound is the donkey's braying (*Luqmān* 31: 18–19).

Promises and Trusts

[Successful are the believers] ... who are faithful to their trusts and to their promises (*al-Mu'minūn* 23: 8).

And be true to every promise – for, verily you will be called to account for every promise which you have made (*al-Isrā'* 17: 34).

Justice

Indeed, We sent Our messengers with evident truth, and We sent down with them the Book and the Balance (of right and wrong), so that people might behave [with each other] with justice (*al-Ḥadīd* 57: 25).

O you who believe, establish justice, being witnesses to the truth, for the sake of God, even though it be against your own selves, or your parents and relatives; whether the person be rich or poor, God's claim takes precedence over either; and, follow not your own desire, lest you swerve from justice (*al-Nisā'* 4: 135).

Never let your enmity for people who barred you from the Holy Mosque move you to commit any excesses against them. Rather, cooperate with one another in good and righteous deeds, and do not cooperate in sinful deeds and injustices (*al-Mā'idah* 5: 2).

Never let your enmity for anyone lead you into the sin of deviating from justice. Always be just: that is closest to being God-fearing (*al-Mā'idah* 5: 8).

The Most Merciful has taught the Qur'an; He has created man, and imparted in him articulate thought and speech. The sun and moon run their appointed courses; and the stars and the trees prostrate themselves; and skies He has raised high, and set the Balance [in all this].

So never transgress in the Balance, and weigh with justice, and skimp not in the Balance (*al-Raḥmān* 55: 1–9).

Woe unto those who give short measure: those who, when they are to receive their due from other people, demand that it be given in full, but when they have to measure or weigh whatever they owe to others, give less than what is due. Do they never think that they shall be raised on an awesome Day, the Day when all people shall stand before the Lord of all the worlds (*al-Muṭaffifīn* 83: 1–6).

Compassion and Generous Giving

Worship and serve God alone and make no gods beside Him; and do good to your parents, the relatives, the orphans, the needy, the neighbour who is a relative, the neighbour who is a stranger, and the companion by your side, and the wayfarer, and to those you rightfully possess; for God loves not the proud and boastful, those who are niggardly and urge others to be niggardly (*al-Nisā'* 4: 36–7).

The freeing of someone's neck from bondage, or the feeding, upon a day of hunger, of an orphan near of kin, or of a needy man rolling in dust: he [who does this] becomes one of those who have faith, and enjoin upon one another patience, and enjoin upon one another compassion to others (*al-Balad* 90: 13–17).

Do you know the one who denies the (Day of) Judgement? It is he who pushes the orphan away, and urges not to feed the needy. Woe, then unto those praying ones, who are heedless of their prayers, who want to be seen and praised, and refuse (to give) even little things in charity (*al-Māʿūn* 107: 1–7).

Those who unjustly devour the property of orphans only fill their bellies with fire, and shall roast in a blazing Fire (*al-Nisāʾ* 4: 10).

Forgiveness

The recompense for an injury is an injury equal thereto; but if a person forgives and makes peace, his reward rests with God; He loves not those who do wrong (*al-Shūrā* 42: 40).

[Your Lord's forgiveness and Paradise as vast as the heavens and earth], are prepared for the God-fearing, who give generously whether in times of plenty or in times of hardship, and hold in check their anger, and pardon their fellow human beings; God loves such doers of good (*Āl ʿImrān* 3: 133–4).

Good and evil can never be equal. Repel (evil) with that which is better, and see how, then, someone between whom and you was enmity shall become a true friend. Yet none is given such goodness except those who are patient; none is given this but the most fortunate (*al-Fuṣṣilat* 41: 34–5).

Patience

No affliction befalls on earth, and neither in your own selves, unless it is [written] in a Book before We bring it into being: verily, all this is easy for God. [Know this] so that you may not grieve for whatever you lose, nor exult over whatever He gives you. God does not love any who, out of self-conceit, act in a boastful manner – those who are niggardly and bid all others to be niggardly (*al-Ḥadīd* 57: 22–4).

Surely We will try you by means of fear, and hunger, and loss of worldly goods, of lives, of produce; but give glad tidings to those who are patient, and, when an affliction befalls them, they say, 'Surely we belong to God, and to Him we shall return' (*al-Baqarah* 2: 155–6).

Rules of Communal Conduct

All believers are but a single brotherhood, so set things right and make peace between your two brothers; and fear God, so that you may receive mercy.

O believers, let no men deride other men, for those may be better than themselves; and, let no women deride other women, for those may be better than themselves; nor defame each other, nor call each other names – evil it is to call by bad names after one has become a believer – and whoever does not repent, it is they who are doing wrong.

O believers, avoid most suspicion, for some suspicion is a sin; do not pry into one another's affairs; and do not speak ill of one another behind your backs – would any of you like to eat the flesh of his dead brother; nay, you would abhor it. Fear God, God accepts repentance and is Mercy-giving (*al-Ḥujurāt* 49: 10–12).

Family

Your Lord has decreed that you shall serve none but Him, and do good to your parents. Should one or both of them reach old age with you, never say 'Ugh' to them, nor scold either of them; but speak to them kindly and respectfully, spread over them the wings of humility and mercy, and say, 'My Lord, have mercy upon them, as they raised me up when I was little' (*al-Isrā'* 17: 23–4).

And We have enjoined upon man goodness towards his parents: his mother bore him by bearing strain upon strain, and his weaning takes two years.

Hence, be thankful to Me and to your parents. With Me is all journey's end. Yet should they endeavour to force you to make gods beside God, of whom you have no knowledge, then do not obey them. But, even then keep them company in this world's life with customary good behaviour, but follow the faith of those who turn towards Me (*Luqmān* 31: 14–15).

Women have rights (over against men) equal to the rights (they owe men) – but men have precedence over them (*al-Baqarah* 2: 228).

Unity of Mankind

O mankind, We have created you all from a male and a female, and have made you into nations and tribes, so that you may identify one another; (otherwise) the noblest among you in the sight of God is (he who is) the most righteous among you; God is All-knowing, All-aware (*al-Ḥujurāt* 49: 13).

9

Life Beyond Life

The Present Life

Know well that the life of this world is but a passing delight and a diversion [from ultimate good], an allurement and a cause of vying with one another in boasting and greed for more and more riches and children.

Its parable is that of rain whose vegetation delights the tillers; but then it soon withers, and you can see it turn yellow; and in the end it crumbles into dust. In the world-to-come there is [waiting for you] either a terrible punishment, or God's forgiveness and His good pleasure; but the life of this world is a joy of self delusion.

So vie with one another in racing to forgiveness from your Lord, and a Paradise as vast as the heavens and the earth (*al-Ḥadīd* 57: 20–1).

Alluring has been made for people the love of desires for women, and children, and heaped up treasures of gold and silver, and horses of high mark, and cattle, and farms. But all this may be enjoyed only in the present life – whereas the best resort is with God.
Say: 'Shall I tell you of better things than these [earthly joys]? For the God-conscious there are, with their Lord, gardens through which waters flow, therein to abide for ever, and pure spouses, and God's good pleasure (*Āl 'Imrān* 3: 14–15).

Verily, that which is with God is the best for you, if you but knew it: all that which is with you is bound to end, whereas all that which is with God is everlasting (*al-Naḥl* 16: 95–6).

And were it not that [with the prospect of boundless riches] all people would become one [evil] community,

We might indeed have given those who deny the All-merciful houses with roofs of silver, and stairways whereon to ascend, for their houses, doors and couches whereon to recline [all of silver], and of gold.

Yet all this would have been nothing but a fleeting enjoyment of life in this world, whereas the life to come awaits the God-conscious with your Lord (*Zukhruf* 43: 33–5).

Those who store up gold and silver, and do not spend them in the way of God – give them the 'good' tidings of a painful punishment, on the day when (their) gold and silver shall be heated in the fire of Hell, and their foreheads and their sides and their backs shall be branded therewith. This is what you stored up for yourselves! Taste, then, your treasures (*al-Tawbah* 9: 34–5).

The parable of those who spend their wealth in the way of God is that of a grain, out of which grow seven ears, in every ear a hundred grains (*al-Baqarah* 2: 261).

The Life to Come

Say: To whom belongs all that is in the heavens and
on earth? Say: To God. He has pledged Himself to do
mercy: He will, therefore, surely gather you all on the
Day of Resurrection – let there be no doubt about it;
yet, those who have squandered their own selves, they
refuse to believe (*al-An'ām* 6: 12).

Wealth and children are an allurement of the
present world; but good deeds, the fruit whereof
endures forever, are better, in the sight of your Lord,
in reward, and as a source of hope.

On the Day We shall set the mountains in motion,
and you will see the earth bare and void; and We shall
gather them all together, so that We would leave not even
one of them behind; and they shall be presented before
your Lord in ranks – 'Now you have come to Us as We
created you the first time; but you thought We would not
fulfil the appointment made with you (to meet Us)?'

And the record [of everyone's deeds] will be laid
open; and you will see the sinners fearful of what is in
it; and they will say, 'Alas for us! What a book is this! It
leaves out nothing, small or great, but takes everything

into account.' Thus they shall find all that they did present before them; and your Lord shall not wrong anyone (*al-Kahf* 18: 46–9).

The great ones [the rich and the powerful] among [every Messenger's] people, rejected the truth and denied the life to come – because We had granted them ease and plenty in their worldly life (and they had become corrupted by it); they said, 'This man is a human being like yourselves, eating what you eat and drinking what you drink. If you pay heed to a human being like yourselves, then you will be losers. What, does he promise you that after you have died and become dust and bones, you shall be brought forth (to a new life)? Far-fetched, far-fetched indeed is what you are promised! There is nothing beyond our life in this world; we die, and we live (but once), and we shall not be raised up. He is nothing but a man who attributes his own invented lies to God, and we are not going to believe him (*al-Mu'minūn* 23: 33–8).

We have not created the heavens and earth and all between them without purpose, though this is what the unbelievers think. Woe to the unbelievers, because of the Fire! Shall We treat those who believe and do righteous deeds in the same manner as those who spread corruption on earth? Shall We treat the God-fearing in the same manner as the wicked? (*Ṣād* 38: 27–8).

O mankind, if you are in doubt about the Resurrection, (consider this:) We created you out of dust, then out of a sperm-drop, then out of a germ-cell, then out of an embryonic lump – complete and yet incomplete – so that We may make things clear to you. And We cause to rest in the wombs what We will [to be born] for an appointed term, then We bring you out infants, then [We let grow] so that you may reach maturity; but some of you die early, and some reach the feeblest old age, when they know nothing of what they once knew so well. And, further, you see the earth dry and lifeless; then, when We send down water upon it, it stirs and swells, and puts forth every kind of lovely plant. This is so, because God alone is the Ultimate Truth, because He brings the dead to life, and because He has power over everything; and because the Hour is bound to come – let there be no doubt about it – and God shall raise up all who are in their graves (*al-Ḥajj* 22: 5–7).

When death comes to one of them, he says, 'My Lord, let me return, let me return to life, so that I act righteously in whatever I have left behind.' Nay, it is but a meaningless word he utters; for, behind them now is the barrier of death until the day they shall be raised up. Then, when the Trumpet will be blown, no ties of kinship will remain between them that day, neither would one be able to take care of another. Then they whose weight of good deeds is heavy in the balance, will attain salvation. But they whose weight is light in the balance, will have squandered their own selves. In Hell will they abide forever (*al-Mu'minūn* 23: 99–103).

To him who desires only this fleeting life We grant him only here and only as much as We please, [giving] only to whomever We will [to give]; but in the end We consign him to Hell.

But as for those who desire the life to come, and strive for it as it ought to be striven for, and are true believers – they are the ones whose strivings all find acceptance and reward (*al-Isrā'* 17: 18–19).

10

Virtue, not Empty
Religiosity

It is not virtue that you turn your faces to the East
or the West, but virtue is if one believes in God, and
the Last Day, and the angels, and the Book, and the
Prophets; and gives away his wealth – out of love
for God – to relatives, and the orphans, and the
needy, and the wayfarer, and the beggars, and for
the freeing of human beings from bondage; and
performs the Prayer, and pays the Alms; and keeps
his promises whenever he makes promises; and
endures with patience misfortune, hardship and
peril; it is they who are true in their faith, and it is
they who are truly God-fearing (*al-Baqarah* 2: 177).

And [God does not love] those who spend their wealth to be seen and praised by people, while they believe neither in God nor in the Last Day (*al-Nisā'* 4: 38).

The flesh of sacrificial animals does not reach God, and neither their blood; but only godliness from you reaches Him (*al-Ḥajj* 22: 37).

And they say, 'None shall enter Paradise unless he be a Jew or a Christian.' These are their wishful beliefs. Say, 'Produce your evidence if what you say is true!'

Nay, whosoever surrenders his whole being unto God, and is a doer of good, shall have his reward from his Lord; on them shall be no fear, neither shall they sorrow (*al-Baqarah* 2: 111–12).

11

Praying to God

If My servants ask you concerning Me, let them know I am very near; I answer the prayer of him who calls, whenever he prays to Me. So let them respond to Me, and believe in Me, so that they might follow the right way (*al-Baqarah* 2: 186).

Your Lord says: Pray to Me, and I shall accept (*Ghāfir* 40: 60).

'Our Lord, take us not to task if we forget or make mistakes. Our Lord, lay not upon us a burden like that which You laid on those before us. Our Lord, make not us bear burdens which we have no strength to bear.

Pardon us, and forgive us, and have mercy on us.

You are our Lord Supreme: Help us against people who deny the truth' (*al-Baqarah* 2: 286).